Dr. Maggie's
Reading Fluency Practice
Jingle Jangles

Written by
Margaret Allen, Ph.D.

Editor: LaDawn Walter
Illustrator: Mary Rojas
Cover Illustrator: Amy Vangsgard
Designer/Production: Moonhee Pak/Carmela Murray
Cover Designer: Barbara Peterson
Art Director: Tom Cochrane
Project Director: Carolea Williams

Table of Contents

Title	Interactive Script	Interactive Mini-Book
Frog Time!	10	11
Nimble Jack and Jill	13	14
Oatmeal Hot	16	17
Charlie Over the Ocean	19	20
Here Is the Beehive	22	23
Kitty Cat and Bowser	25	26
Brother John and Sister Kate	28	29
Bought Me a Cat	31	33
Two Little Bluebirds	35	36
Up the Sea Rises	38	39
Fooba-Wooba John	41	43
John the Rabbit	45	46
Go Away Mr. Rain Cloud!	48	49
Noble Duke of York	51	52
Sandwich Favorite	54	56
By the Barnyard Gate	58	59
When the Boat Comes In	61	62
Did You Find My Cow?	64	66
Nobody Likes Me!	68	69
Michael Finnegan	71	72
She'll Be Coming 'Round the Mountain	74	77
The Smile of the Crocodile	79	80
Bill Grogan's Goat	82	84
Big Rock Candy Mountain	86	87
Way Down South	89	91
The Humpty Dumpty Rap	93	95
A Shoe-Full!	97	98
Miss Mary Mack and Friends	100	102
Old Chisholm Trail	104	106
Hush, My Children	108	110
Mr. Frog Went Courtin'	112	114
Jack and Jill's Motion Commotion	116	119

Dear Teachers,

What an exciting time to be a teacher! With the *No Child Left Behind* Act and *Put Reading First,* we have research building blocks for teaching children how to improve their reading skills and a national initiative to support this effort.

Jingle Jangles features 32 interactive scripts and mini-books based on familiar songs and chants that help children practice something that is often overlooked when teaching them to read—fluency. Fluency is the ability to read text accurately, quickly, and naturally. Fluency is not a specific stage of reading development at which readers can read all words in text quickly, easily, and naturally. Rather, it continues to change depending on what is being read, the child's familiarity with the words in the text, and with the amount of practice he or she has reading a particular text. It is critical to teach fluency because it is the bridge between word recognition and comprehension.

Research has confirmed that the more children practice reading, the better they read. Also, the more children read familiar text, the more automatically they recognize words. The more automatically children recognize words, the more fluently they read. And, the more fluent children become, the more natural, expressive, and confident they are in their reading. When children do not have to concentrate on decoding words, they can focus their attention on understanding the text, which in turn leads to greater comprehension, understanding, and learning.

Jingle Jangles provides this necessary element of repeated reading practice in a fun and interactive way. In this resource, you will find 32 songs and chants that are most appropriate for kindergarten through second-grade children. I have selected them from America's common oral tradition or written them myself. I have also adapted these songs and chants into 8-page reproducible mini-books. You will find the titles ordered by skill level (from easiest to most difficult) in the Table of Contents. You may find that some of the mini-books found early on in the order of skill level have a lot of words or more sentences than mini-books found later on. These are considered to be less difficult because of the amount of repeated text verses the amount of new vocabulary words being introduced in later mini-books. In addition to the scripts and mini-books, you will find a variety of exciting strategies and reproducibles to help you implement these interactive reading selections in meaningful ways.

So, my fellow teachers, read, read, and read again. Make reading meaningful, make it entertaining, and make it fun!

Sincerely,

Dr. Margaret Allen, Ph.D. (Dr. Maggie)

Setting the Stage

Children develop reading fluency when they have multiple opportunities to orally reread the same passage. The challenge is to provide this repeated reading practice while maintaining children's interest. The interactive scripts and mini-books in *Jingle Jangles* provide interesting, patterned text that allows an opportunity for you to model fluent reading to children and for children to practice rereading orally. In addition, the interactive reading strategies and reproducibles provide a fun and exciting stage for the scripts and mini-books not only to come alive but to stay alive. This keeps children's level of interest high throughout several "takes" of the same text.

Interactive Scripts

This resource contains 32 interactive scripts that are based on fun and familiar songs and chants. They provide text with rhyme, rhythm, and meaning that helps children make the transition from merely decoding words to reading fluently and with expression.

Directions

Choose an interactive script that matches the reading level and interest of the children in your class. Copy it onto chart or butcher paper, or make a transparency of it for the whole class to read. Also, make copies of the original reproducible, and give one to each child. (Copy the scripts on various colors of paper to help children distinguish between them.)

Model reading the script during the Morning Message, as a shared reading warm-up, or during your Reader's Workshop at the beginning of the week to introduce the text to children. Then, choose a different interactive reading strategy from the Ready, Set, Read! section (see pages 7–9) for each day of the week to have children practice rereading the text. In addition to these strategies, continue rereading the text with children at random times throughout the week. Use them during "sponge activity time," before lunch or recess, as children line up to leave the room at the end of the day, or during a class "wiggle time" where they get up and dance as they read the song. The goal is to have children read, read, and read again during every spare moment of the day so that they are very familiar with the text and comfortable reading it.

Interactive Mini-Books

There are 32 interactive mini-books, one for each script, in this resource. Each mini-book includes a cover and seven pages of text with interesting and supportive illustrations. Encourage children to read the mini-books silently or orally, independently or with a partner, at school or at home to continue to build their confidence and fluency.

Directions

Once children have become familiar and confident reading the script text, it is time to introduce the mini-book that accompanies the script. Make copies of the 8-page mini-book, cut apart the pages, and staple them together. Give one mini-book to each child. Invite children to color their mini-book and practice reading it independently or with a partner. Place the mini-books in a learning center or reading folders (see below), or have children take them home to enjoy reading practice with family members. Also, place a copy of each mini-book in the classroom library so there is always a copy available at school.

Reading Folder

Give each child a folder with pockets and three brads down the center. Give children a piece of blank paper to create a cover page. Invite children to write their name on this cover page and decorate it. Glue each child's cover page to the front of his or her folder. Three-hole punch children's script reproducibles. Help children place the reproducibles in the center of the folder with the brads and put their mini-books in one of the pockets. Have children read their scripts and mini-books during independent work time, while waiting for a new activity to begin, or at home with family members.

What's My Role?

In the back of this resource, you will find a variety of reproducibles that represent the themes and character roles of the scripts and mini-books. (Some of the role titles may be used more than once.) Make the following props to create excitement to enhance reading practice, to specify each child's role in the script, and to help children feel more associated with the character whose part they are reading. Refer to the top of each reading script for the list of roles and the page numbers of corresponding reproducibles.

Directions

Necklaces: Choose a script, and copy the corresponding reproducibles. Punch holes where indicated, insert a piece of yarn in each hole, and tie together the ends to make a necklace. Place these necklaces over children's heads to identify which role a child is reading.

Headbands: Choose a script, and copy the corresponding reproducibles. Cut long strips of construction paper. Staple the two ends of each piece of paper together to create a headband. Color the reproducible pieces that represent various roles, cut them out, and staple each one to a construction paper headband. Have children wear the headbands while reading the script and mini-book.

Puppets: Choose a script, and copy the corresponding reproducibles. Color and cut out each piece. Staple each piece to a tongue depressor, craft stick, or paper bag to create a puppet. Have children use the puppets while reading the script and mini-book.

Costumes: Have children make costumes from art supplies (e.g., construction paper, sequins, glitter, markers, stickers). Invite children to wear the costumes as they read their roles in the script.

Ready, Set, Read!

There are a variety of ways children can practice rereading the scripts to gain fluency while maintaining their interest. The following variations can be used with most scripts. However, scripts with two or four reading parts or the "Solo with Echo" are better implemented in a partner or group setting. Scripts with three reading parts or more than four reading parts can only be used in a group setting.

Partner Reading
(For scripts that include two or four reading roles and the Solo with Echo)

In partner reading, there are two specific reading parts to the script, such as Reader 1 and Reader 2. Partners can have similar reading levels or opposite reading levels. If the partners' levels are similar, either child can read either role. If the partners' levels are opposite, the stronger reader should read the more difficult text. With a script that consists of four roles, have each partner read the parts for two separate roles. To help children concentrate better and hear their partner more clearly, have them place their chair backs in opposite directions so that they are sitting ear to ear. While one child reads his or her part, the other child follows along on his or her copy and then reads the next part. Children complete the entire reading this way.

Group Reading
(For scripts that include two, three, four, or more reading roles or the Solo with Echo)

Scripts that include two or more parts can be read in a small- or large-group setting. In a small-group setting, divide the class into smaller groups that consist of the same number of children as there are roles. For example, if a script has four roles, then a class of 20 children would be divided into five groups of four. Then, one child at a time would read his or her part within the small group. (All five groups would be reading within their own group at the same time.) On the contrary, in a large-group setting, divide the class into as many groups as there are roles. For example, a class reading a script with three roles would be split into three large groups. Each group of children would read their part aloud together as a group to the rest of the class. Solo with Echo reading scripts are an excellent way to support struggling readers, second-language learners, or kindergartners. In Solo with Echo reading, a strong reader, parent, older child, or teacher reads the solo part to the class or a partner, which allows for modeled fluent reading. Then, the whole class or partner repeats the text as an echo.

Taped Reading
(For all scripts)

Have a teacher, parent volunteer, or fluent reader read each script into a tape recorder. Place the tape along with copies of the script in the Listening Center. The first few times children listen to a script on tape, have them point to the words as they listen. Then, when children are comfortable, invite them to read along as they listen to the script on tape. Children can complete this activity independently or in a group. Assign separate roles if a group of children is listening to the tape at one time.

Reader's Theater
(For all scripts)

Have children practice their assigned roles several times until they are fluent and reading them with confidence. Invite children to create masks and/or costumes that represent the role they are reading. Then, have them wear their costumes when they read the script to the rest of the class, other classrooms, and/or parents. As a variation to Reader's Theater, have children work in groups or pairs to "sing" their own version of the songs/chants. Encourage them to experiment with varied voice levels, intonation, chanting styles, or musical styles.

Buddy Reading

(For all scripts)

Find an upper-grade class (about two to three grades higher than your own) to become "Study Buddies" with your class. Pair up a child from your class with a child in the upper-grade class. Invite your study buddy class to your classroom one to three times a week to read with your children for about 10–15 minutes. Have each pair of study buddies read the scripts together. Depending on the ability of each reader, children can take turns reading various roles in the script. This is a fun way for children to hear fluent readers and for classes to interact with one another. The younger children look up to their older study buddies, and the older children delight in hearing the younger children read.

Lead Reader

(For scripts that include three, four, or more reading roles or the Solo with Echo)

Use the Leader reproducible (page 124) as a special reward for an improved reader. Have children sit in a circle. Choose a child to lead the class in a group reading. Invite the lead reader to read the first line of the script. Have the child to the leader's right read the second line, the third child read the next line, and so forth. Continue around the circle with each child reading one line. When the script is finished, have the lead reader repeat the first line of the script, and have children repeat the steps above. Encourage them to read faster each time they repeat the script. As a variation, have the lead reader carry a special wand. Invite the lead reader to read the first line and then touch another child to read the second line. Have the lead reader continue this until the entire script has been read.

Roles: Child 1, Child 2, Frog 1, and Frog 2

Reproducible: Page 121

Frog Time!
By Dr. Maggie

Child 1
Glub! Glub!
Frog time!
Green
Brown
Big
Little
Jumpy
Bumpy
We like

Child 2
Croak! Croak!
Frog time!
frogs.
frogs.
frogs.
frogs.
frogs.
frogs.
frogs!

Frog 1
Gulp! Gulp!
Bug time!
Flying
Crawling
Jumping
Swimming
Juicy
Tasty
We like

Frog 2
Yum! Yum!
Bug time!
bugs.
bugs.
bugs.
bugs.
bugs.
bugs.
bugs!

Frog Time!

By Dr. Maggie

Name_____

Jingle Jangles © 2004 Creative Teaching Press

Croak! Croak!

Glub! Glub!
Croak! Croak!
Frog time!
Frog time!

1

Green frogs.
Brown frogs.
Big frogs.
Little frogs.

2

Jumpy frogs.
Bumpy frogs.
We like frogs!

3

Gulp! Gulp!
Yum! Yum!
Bug time!
Bug time!

4

Flying bugs.
Crawling bugs.

5

Jumping bugs.
Swimming bugs.

6

Juicy bugs.
Tasty bugs.
We like bugs!

7

Roles: Solo and Echo Reader(s)

Reproducible: Page 122

Nimble Jack and Jill

Adapted by Dr. Maggie

Solo Reader

Jack be nimble.
Jack be quick.
Jack jump over
the candlestick.
Jump, Jack, jump!

Jill be nimble.
Jump it, too.
Jack jumped high
and so can you.
Jump, Jill, jump!

Jump, jump, Jack.
Jump, jump, Jill.
Jump, jump, Jack and Jill!

Echo Reader(s)

Jack be nimble.
Jack be quick.
Jack jump over
the candlestick.
Jump, Jack, jump!

Jill be nimble.
Jump it, too.
Jack jumped high
and so can you.
Jump, Jill, jump!

Jump, jump, Jack.
Jump, jump, Jill.
Jump, jump, Jack and Jill!

Nimble Jack and Jill

Adapted by Dr. Maggie

Name_____

Jack be nimble.
Jack be quick.

1

Jack jump over the candlestick.

2

Jump, Jack, jump!
Jump, Jack, jump!

3

Jill be nimble.
Jump it, too.

4

Jack jumped high and so can you.

5

Jump, Jill, jump!
Jump, Jill, jump!

6

Jump, jump, Jack.
Jump, jump, Jill.
Jump, jump, Jack and Jill!

7

Roles: Reader 1 and Reader 2

Reproducible: Page 123

Oatmeal Hot

By Dr. Maggie

Reader 1	Reader 2
Oatmeal	hot.
Oatmeal	cold.
Oatmeal	in the pot
nine days	old.
Some like it	hot.
Some like it	cold.
But no one likes it	in the pot
nine days	old!
Oatmeal	hot.
Oatmeal	cold.
Oatmeal	in the pot
nine days	old.
Some like it	with milk.
Some like it	with tea.
But no one likes it	nine days old!
Not YOU,	and not ME!

Oatmeal Hot

By Dr. Maggie

Name_____

Jingle Jangles © 2004 Creative Teaching Press

Oatmeal hot.
Oatmeal cold.
Oatmeal in the pot
nine days old.

1

Some like it hot.
Some like it cold.

2

Yuck! Nine days old!

But no one likes it in the pot
nine days old!

3

Oatmeal hot.
Oatmeal cold.
Oatmeal in the pot
nine days old.

4

Some like it with milk.
Some like it with tea.

5

Yuck!
Nine days old!

But no one likes it
nine days old!

6

Not YOU,
and not ME!

7

Roles: Solo and Echo Reader(s)

Reproducible: Page 122

Charlie Over the Ocean

Adapted by Dr. Maggie

Solo Reader

Charlie over the ocean.
Charlie over the sea.
Charlie caught a lobster,
but he didn't catch me!

Charlie over the ocean.
Charlie over the sea.
Charlie caught a tuna,
but he didn't catch me!

Charlie over the ocean.
Charlie over the sea.
Charlie caught a bad cold,
but he didn't give it to me!

Echo Reader(s)

Charlie over the ocean.
Charlie over the sea.
Charlie caught a lobster,
but he didn't catch me!

Charlie over the ocean.
Charlie over the sea.
Charlie caught a tuna,
but he didn't catch me!

Charlie over the ocean.
Charlie over the sea.
Charlie caught a bad cold,
but he didn't give it to me!

Charlie Over the Ocean

Adapted by Dr. Maggie

Name_____

Jingle Jangles © 2004 Creative Teaching Press

**Charlie over the ocean.
Charlie over the sea.**

1

**Charlie caught a lobster,
but he didn't catch me!**

2

**Charlie over the ocean.
Charlie over the sea.**

3

Charlie caught a tuna,
but he didn't catch me!

4

Charlie over the ocean.
Charlie over the sea.

5

Charlie caught a bad cold, but . . .

6

. . . he didn't give it to me!

7

Here Is the Beehive

Adapted by Dr. Maggie

Solo Reader

Here is the beehive.
Where are the bees?
Hidden away
where nobody sees.

Watch to see them
come out of the hive.
Buzzzz!
1-2-3-4-5.

Echo Reader(s)

Here is the beehive.
Where are the bees?
Hidden away
where nobody sees.

Watch to see them
come out of the hive.
Buzzzz!
1-2-3-4-5.

Here Is the Beehive

Adapted by Dr. Maggie

Name_____

Jingle Jangles © 2004 Creative Teaching Press

Here is the beehive.

1

Where are the bees?

2

Hidden away

3

where nobody sees.

4

Watch to see them

5

come out of the hive.

6

Buzzzz!
1-2-3-4-5.

7

Roles: Reader 1, Reader 2, Dog, and Cat

Reproducible: Page 123

Kitty Cat and Bowser

By Dr. Maggie

Reader 1

Bowser went outside.
Bowser saw Kitty Cat.
Trouble?
Let's find out.

Reader 2

Kitty Cat went outside.
Kitty Cat saw Bowser.
Maybe not!
Let's do.

Dog

Bowwow. Hello!
I am Bowser.
Do you know what I like to do?
I like to eat.
I like to sleep.
I like to run.
I like to play.
And, I like to chase cats!
Yes, YOU!

Cat

Meow. Hello!
I am Kitty Cat.
No.
Me, too!
Me, too!
Me, too!
Me, too!
Not ME!
H-E-L-P!

Kitty Cat and Bowser

By Dr. Maggie

Name_____

Bowser went outside.
Kitty Cat went outside.
Bowser saw Kitty Cat.
Kitty Cat saw Bowser.

1

Bowwow!

Meow!

Bowwow. Hello!
Meow. Hello!
I am Bowser.
I am Kitty Cat.

2

Kitty Cat

Bowser

Do you know what I like to do?
No.
I like to eat.
Me, too!

3

I like to sleep.
Me, too!
4

I like to run.
Me, too!
5

I like to play.
Me, too!
6

And, I like to chase cats!
Not ME!
Yes, YOU!
H-E-L-P!
7

Roles: Reader 1 and Reader 2

Reproducible: Page 123

Brother John and Sister Kate

Adapted by Dr. Maggie

Reader 1

Are you sleeping,
Brother John?
Morning bells
Morning bells
Ding, ding, dong.

I'm not sleeping,
Sister Kate.
Time to go
Time to go
Can't be late!

Reader 2

Are you sleeping,
Brother John?
are ringing.
are ringing.
Ding, ding, dong.

I'm not sleeping,
Sister Kate.
to school now.
to school now.
Can't be late!

Brother John and Sister Kate

Adapted by Dr. Maggie

Name_____

Jingle Jangles © 2004 Creative Teaching Press

Are you sleeping,
Are you sleeping,

1

Brother John?
Brother John?

2

Morning bells are ringing.
Morning bells are ringing.
Ding, ding, dong.
Ding, ding, dong.

3

I'm not sleeping,
I'm not sleeping,

4

Sister Kate.
Sister Kate.

5

Time to go to school now.
Time to go to school now.

6

Can't be late!
Can't be late!

7

Roles: Reader 1, Reader 2, and Solos—Cat, Hen, Duck, Dog

Reproducibles: Pages 123 and 126

Bought Me a Cat

Adapted by Dr. Maggie

Reader 1: I bought me a cat,
Reader 2: and the cat pleased me.

Reader 1: I fed my cat
Reader 2: under yonder tree. Cat went…

Cat: Fiddle-i-fee.

Reader 1: I bought me a hen,
Reader 2: and the hen pleased me.

Reader 1: I fed my hen
Reader 2: under yonder tree. Hen went…

Hen: Chimmy-chuck, chimmy-chuck.

Reader 1: And the cat went…
Cat: Fiddle-i-fee.

Reader 1: I bought me a duck,
Reader 2: and the duck pleased me.

Reader 1: I fed my duck
Reader 2: under yonder tree. Duck went…

Duck: Quack, quack.

Reader 1: Hen went…
Hen: Chimmy-chuck, chimmy-chuck.
Reader 2: And the cat went…
Cat: Fiddle-i-fee.

Reader 1: I bought me a dog,
Reader 2: and the dog pleased me.

Reader 1: I fed my dog
Reader 2: under yonder tree. Dog went…

Dog: Bowwow.

Reader 1: Duck went…
Duck: Quack, quack.
Reader 2: Hen went…
Hen: Chimmy-chuck, chimmy-chuck.

Reader 1: And the cat went…
Cat: Fiddle-i-fee!

Fiddle-i-fee!

Bought Me a Cat

Adapted by Dr. Maggie

Name_____

I bought me a cat,
and the cat pleased me.
I fed my cat under yonder tree.
Cat went . . . Fiddle-i-fee.

1

I bought me a hen,
and the hen pleased me.
I fed my hen under yonder tree.
Hen went . . .
Chimmy-chuck, chimmy-chuck.

2

Fiddle-i-fee!

And the cat went . . . Fiddle-i-fee.

3

I bought me a duck,
and the duck pleased me.
I fed my duck under yonder tree.
Duck went . . . Quack, quack.

4

Hen went . . .
Chimmy-chuck, chimmy-chuck.
And the cat went . . . Fiddle-i-fee.

5

I bought me a dog,
and the dog pleased me.
I fed my dog under yonder tree.
Dog went . . . Bowwow.

6

Duck went . . . Quack, quack.
Hen went . . .
Chimmy-chuck, chimmy-chuck.
And the cat went . . . Fiddle-i-fee!

7

Roles: Reader 1 and Reader 2

Reproducible: Page 123

Two Little Bluebirds

Adapted by Dr. Maggie

Reader 1
Two little bluebirds
One named Jack.
Fly away, Jack.
Come back, Jack.

Two little blackbirds
One named Sal.
Fly away, Sal.
Come back, Sal.

Two little red birds
One named Dan.
Fly away, Dan.
Come back, Dan.

Six pretty birds
Don't fly away!

Reader 2
sitting on a hill.
And one named Jill.
Fly away, Jill.
Come back, Jill.

sitting on a fence.
And one named Spence.
Fly away, Spence.
Come back, Spence.

sitting in a tree.
And one named Dee.
Fly away, Dee.
Come back, Dee.

sitting near me.
Stay with me!

Two Little Bluebirds

Adapted by Dr. Maggie

Name_____

Jingle Jangles © 2004 Creative Teaching Press

Two little bluebirds
sitting on a hill.
One named Jack.
And one named Jill.

1

Fly away, Jack.
Fly away, Jill.
Come back, Jack.
Come back, Jill.

2

Two little blackbirds
sitting on a fence.
One named Sal.
And one named Spence.

3

Fly away, Sal.
Fly away, Spence.
Come back, Sal.
Come back, Spence.

4

Two little red birds
sitting in a tree.
One named Dan.
And one named Dee.

5

Fly away, Dan.
Fly away, Dee.
Come back, Dan.
Come back, Dee.

6

Six pretty birds sitting near me.
Don't fly away!
Stay with me!

7

Up the Sea Rises

Adapted by Dr. Maggie

Reader 1	Reader 2
Heave, ho!	And up the sea rises.
Heave, ho!	And up the sea rises.
Heave, ho!	And up the sea rises.
Early in	the morning.
What will we do	with a lazy sailor?
What will we do	with a lazy sailor?
What will we do	with a lazy sailor?
Early in	the morning.
Make the sailor work	till up the sea rises.
Make the sailor work	till up the sea rises.
Make the sailor work	till up the sea rises.
Early in	the morning.
Pull on the anchor	and up the sea rises.
Pull on the anchor	and up the sea rises.
Pull on the anchor	and up the sea rises.
Early in	the morning.
Pull on the rope	and hoist the mainsail.
Pull on the rope	and hoist the mainsail.
Pull on the rope	and hoist the mainsail.
Early in	the morning.
Heave, ho!	And up the sea rises.
Heave, ho!	And up the sea rises.
Heave, ho!	And up the sea rises.
Early in	the morning.

Up the Sea Rises

Adapted by Dr. Maggie

Name_____

Jingle Jangles © 2004 Creative Teaching Press

Heave, ho! And up the sea rises.
Heave, ho! And up the sea rises.
Heave, ho! And up the sea rises.
Early in the morning.

1

What will we do
with a lazy sailor?
What will we do
with a lazy sailor?
What will we do
with a lazy sailor?
Early in the morning.

2

Make the sailor work
till up the sea rises.
Make the sailor work
till up the sea rises.
Make the sailor work
till up the sea rises.
Early in the morning.

3

Pull on the anchor and
up the sea rises.
Pull on the anchor and
up the sea rises.
Pull on the anchor and
up the sea rises.
Early in the morning.

4

Pull on the rope and
hoist the mainsail.
Pull on the rope and
hoist the mainsail.
Pull on the rope and
hoist the mainsail.
Early in the morning.

5

Heave, ho! And up the sea rises.
Heave, ho! And up the sea rises.
Heave, ho! And up the sea rises.

6

Early in the morning.

7

Fooba–Wooba John

Adapted by Dr. Maggie

Group 1: Foo-ba-woo-ba, foo-ba-woo-ba.

Group 2: Saw a snail chase a whale.

Group 1: Foo-ba-woo-ba, foo-ba-woo-ba.

Group 2: Saw a snail chase a whale
all around a water pail.

Group 1: Hey, John! Ho, John!

Group 2: Hey, John! Ho, John!

Group 1: Foo-ba-woo-ba, John.
Foo-ba-woo-ba, foo-ba-woo-ba.

Group 2: Saw a frog chase a dog.

Group 1: Foo-ba-woo-ba, foo-ba-woo-ba.

Group 2: Saw a frog chase a dog
all around a hollow log.

Group 1: Hey, John! Ho, John!

Group 2: Hey, John! Ho, John!

Group 1: Foo-ba-woo-ba, John.
Foo-ba-woo-ba, foo-ba-woo-ba.

Group 2: Saw a flea kick a tree.

Group 1: Foo-ba-woo-ba, foo-ba-woo-ba.

Group 2: Saw a flea kick a tree
in the middle of the sea.

Group 1: Hey, John! Ho, John!

Group 2: Hey, John! Ho, John!

Group 1: Foo-ba-woo-ba, John.
Foo-ba-woo-ba, foo-ba-woo-ba.

Group 2: Heard a cow say "meow."

Group 1: Foo-ba-woo-ba, foo-ba-woo-ba.

Group 2: Heard a cow say "meow."
Then I heard it say "bowwow."

Group 1: Hey, John! Ho, John!

Group 2: Hey, John! Ho, John!

Group 1: Foo-ba-woo-ba, John.

Fooba–Wooba John

Adapted by Dr. Maggie

Name_____

Jingle Jangles © 2004 Creative Teaching Press

Foo-ba-woo-ba, foo-ba-woo-ba.
Saw a snail chase a whale.
Saw a snail chase a whale
all around a water pail.

1

Hey, John! Ho, John!
Hey, John! Ho, John!
Foo-ba-woo-ba, John.

2

Foo-ba-woo-ba, foo-ba-woo-ba.
Saw a frog chase a dog.
Saw a frog chase a dog
all around a hollow log.

3

Hey, John! Ho, John!
Hey, John! Ho, John!
Foo-ba-woo-ba, John.

4

Foo-ba-woo-ba, foo-ba-woo-ba.
Saw a flea kick a tree.
Saw a flea kick a tree
in the middle of the sea.

5

Hey, John! Ho, John!
Hey, John! Ho, John!
Foo-ba-woo-ba, John.

6

Heard a cow say "meow."
Then I heard it say "bowwow."
Hey, John! Ho, John!
Foo-ba-woo-ba, John.

7

Roles: Farmer and Rabbit

Reproducible: Page 122

John the Rabbit

Adapted by Dr. Maggie

Farmer	**Rabbit**
Oh, John the Rabbit.	Oh, yes!
Oh, John the Rabbit.	Oh, yes!
You have a mighty bad habit	Oh, yes!
of going in my garden	Oh, yes!
and eating up my peas	Oh, yes!
and cutting down my cabbage.	Oh, yes!
You ate tomatoes	Oh, yes!
and sweet potatoes.	Oh, yes!
And when I live	Oh, yes!
to see next fall,	Oh, yes!
I won't plant	Oh, yes!
a garden at all!	Oh, NO!

John the Rabbit

Adapted by Dr. Maggie

Name_____

Oh, John the Rabbit.
Oh, yes!
Oh, John the Rabbit.
Oh, yes!

1

You have a mighty bad habit
Oh, yes!

2

of going in my garden
Oh, yes!

3

and eating up my peas
Oh, yes!
and cutting down my cabbage.
Oh, yes!

4

You ate tomatoes
Oh, yes!
and sweet potatoes.
Oh, yes!

5

And when I live
Oh, yes!
to see next fall,
Oh, yes!

6

I won't plant
Oh, yes!
a garden at all!
Oh, NO!

7

Roles: Reader 1 and Reader 2

Reproducible: Page 123

Go Away Mr. Rain Cloud!

Adapted by Dr. Maggie

Reader 1	Reader 2
Rain, rain	go away.
Come again	another day.
All my friends	want to play.
We want	to climb.
We want	to run.
We want	to swing.
We want	to have fun!
So, Mr. Rain Cloud . . .	Please, Mr. Rain Cloud . . .
Go, go!	Go away.
Come again	another day.
All my friends	want to play.

Jingle Jangles © 2004 Creative Teaching Press

Go Away Mr. Rain Cloud!

Adapted by Dr. Maggie

Name_____

Jingle Jangles © 2004 Creative Teaching Press

**Rain, rain go away.
Come again another day.**

1

All my friends want to play.

2

**We want to climb.
We want to run.**

3

We want to swing.
We want to have fun!

4

So, Mr. Rain Cloud . . .
Please, Mr. Rain Cloud . . .

5

Go, go!
Go away.
Come again another day.

6

All my friends want to play.

7

Roles: Reader 1 and Reader 2

Reproducible: Page 123

Noble Duke of York

Adapted by Dr. Maggie

Reader 1

The noble Duke of York
He marched them up the hill.
When you're up,
And when you're down,
But when you're only
you're neither up

The royal Queen of Hearts
She marched them up the hill.
When you're up,
And when you're down,
But when you're only
you're neither up

The Duke's ten thousand men
For tarts, they'd march right up a hill.
When you're up,
And when you're down,
But when you're only
you're neither up

Reader 2

had ten thousand men.
Then he marched them down again.
you're up.
you're down.
halfway up,
nor down!

baked ten thousand tarts.
Then she marched right down again.
you're up.
you're down.
halfway up,
nor down!

were grateful once again.
Then march right down again.
you're up.
you're down.
halfway up,
nor down!

Noble Duke of York

Adapted by Dr. Maggie

Name_____

Jingle Jangles © 2004 Creative Teaching Press

The noble Duke of York
had ten thousand men.
He marched them up the hill.
Then he marched them
down again.

1

When you're up, you're up.
And when you're down,
you're down.
But when you're
only halfway up,
you're neither up nor down!

2

The royal Queen of Hearts
baked ten thousand tarts.
She marched them up the hill.
Then she marched right
down again.

3

When you're up, you're up.
And when you're down,
you're down.
But when you're
only halfway up,
you're neither up nor down!

4

The Duke's ten thousand men
were grateful once again.
For tarts, they'd march
right up a hill.
Then march right down again.

5

When you're up, you're up.
And when you're down,
you're down.
But when you're only
halfway up . . .

6

you're neither up nor down!

7

Roles: Group 1, Group 2, Group 3, Group A, Group B, and Group C

Reproducibles: Pages 124 and 125

Sandwich Favorite

Adapted by Dr. Maggie

Group 1: I'm hungry!

Group 2: So am I!

Group 3: Let's make a sandwich.

Group 1: What kind shall we make?

Group 2: I don't know. How about ham and cheese?

Group 3: I know! Let's make our favorite sandwich—peanut butter and jelly!

Group 1: Sounds delicious to me!

Group 2: First we'll need some peanut butter.

Group A: A can of peanuts on a railroad track.

Group B: The wind rushing, flutter, flutter.

Group C: Along comes a great big locomotive.

Group A: Choo! Choo!

Group B: Peanut butter!

Group 1: Good. We have the peanut butter.
Now we need the jelly.

Group 2: I have the jelly—grape jelly.

Group 3: Here's the bread. Our favorite
sandwich is on the way!

Group A: Peanut, peanut butter.

Group B: Jelly, jelly.

Group C: First you take the peanut butter,
and you spread it, spread it.

Group A: Next you take the jelly,

Group B: and you spread it, spread it.

Group C: Then you take the pieces,
and marry 'em, marry 'em.

Group A: Last you take the sandwich,

Group B: and you eat it, eat it!

Group C: Peanut, peanut butter.
Jelly, jelly. Yummmm!

**Groups
1, 2, 3:** Yummmm! Peanut butter and jelly!

**Groups
A, B, C:** That was delicious!

Sandwich Favorite

Adapted by Dr. Maggie

Name_____

I'm hungry! So am I!
Let's make our
favorite sandwich—
peanut butter and jelly!
First we'll need some
peanut butter.

1

A can of peanuts on
a railroad track.
The wind rushing, flutter, flutter.
Along comes a great
big locomotive.
Choo! Choo! Peanut butter!

2

Good.
We have the peanut butter.
Now we need the grape jelly
and bread.
Our favorite sandwich
is on the way!

3

Peanut, peanut butter.
Jelly, jelly.
First you take the peanut butter,
and you spread it, spread it.

4

Next you take the jelly,
and you spread it, spread it.
Then you take the pieces
and marry 'em, marry 'em.

5

Last you take the sandwich,
and you eat it, eat it!
Peanut, peanut butter.
Jelly, jelly.

6

Yummmm!
Peanut butter and jelly!
That was delicious!

7

By the Barnyard Gate

Adapted by Dr. Maggie

Roles: Child 1, Child 2, Group A, Group B, and Group C

Reproducibles: Pages 121 and 125

Child 1: Here we are at the farm.
Look at that big red barn!
Gee! Listen to all of those animals.

Child 2: Yes! What a noisy place!
Let's listen to what they are saying!

Group A: I had a little rooster by the barnyard gate.

Group B: And that little rooster was my playmate.

Group C: And that little rooster went "Cock-a-doodle-doo!
Cock-a-doodle, cock-a-doodle, cock-a-doodle-doo!"

Group A: I had a little pig by the barnyard gate.

Group B: And that little pig was my playmate.

Group C: And that little pig went "Oink, oink, oink!
Oinkety, oink, oink. Oinkety, oink, oink.
Oink, oink, oink!"

Group A: I had a little duck by the barnyard gate.

Group B: And that little duck was my playmate.

Group C: And that little duck went "Quack, quack, quack!
Quackety, quack, quack. Quackety, quack, quack.
Quack, quack, quack!"

Child 1: I like all of the animals, noise and all.
Don't you?

Child 2: Yes, I do. What a fun day at the farm!

By the Barnyard Gate

Adapted by Dr. Maggie

Name_____

Jingle Jangles © 2004 Creative Teaching Press

Here we are at the farm.
Look at that big red barn!
Look at all of those animals.
What a noisy place! Listen!

1

I had a little rooster
by the barnyard gate.
And that little rooster
was my playmate.

2

Cock-a-doodle-doo!

And that little rooster went
"Cock-a-doodle-doo!
Cock-a-doodle, cock-a-doodle,
cock-a-doodle-doo!"

3

I had a little pig
by the barnyard gate.
And that little pig
was my playmate.

4

And that little pig went
"Oink, oink, oink!
Oinkety, oink, oink.
Oinkety, oink, oink.
Oink, oink, oink!"

5

I had a little duck
by the barnyard gate.
And that little duck
was my playmate.

6

And that little duck went
"Quack, quack, quack!
Quackety, quack, quack.
Quackety, quack, quack.
Quack, quack, quack!"

7

When the Boat Comes In

Adapted by Dr. Maggie

Child 1: It's almost bedtime.

Child 2: I know. And Daddy is going to work.

Child 1: I wish he didn't have to sail so far away.

Child 2: I know. But that is where the fish are.

Child 1: Let's ask him to sing to us before he goes.

Child 2: Good idea! Daddy, please sing us a song.

Dad: Okay, but then you have to go to sleep.
My grandpa sang this song to me when I was little.
He was a fisherman—just like my daddy and just like me!

Group 1
Dance to your daddy,
Dance to your daddy,
You shall have a fish
And you shall have a haddock

Dance to your daddy,
Dance to your daddy,
You shall have a fishy
You shall have a fishy

Group 2
my little children.
my little men.
and you shall have a fin.
when the boat comes in.

my brave little laddies.
my little men.
in a little dishy.
when the boat comes in.

When the Boat Comes In

Adapted by Dr. Maggie

Name_____

It's almost bedtime.
I know.
And Daddy is going to work.

1

I wish he didn't have
to sail so far away.
I know.
But that is where the fish are.

2

Let's ask him to sing to us
before he goes.
Good idea!
Daddy, please sing us a song.

3

Dance to your daddy,
my little children.
Dance to your daddy,
my little men.

4

You shall have a fish
and you shall have a fin.
And you shall have a haddock
when the boat comes in.

5

Dance to your daddy,
my brave little laddies.
Dance to your daddy,
my little men.

6

You shall have a fishy
in a little dishy.
You shall have a fishy
when the boat comes in.

7

Roles: Group 1 and Group 2

Reproducible: Page 124

Did You Find My Cow?

Adapted by Dr. Maggie

Group 1	Group 2
Did you find my cow?	Yes, ma'am.
Could you tell me how?	Yes, ma'am.
Where did you find her?	Down in a ditch.
Where did you find her?	Down in a ditch.
Did her legs seem hurt?	Yes, ma'am.
Were they covered with dirt?	Yes, ma'am.
What did she say?	Moo, moo, moo.
What did she say?	Moo, moo, moo.
Did you pet her good?	Yes, ma'am.
Did you pet her like you should?	Yes, ma'am.

Group 1	**Group 2**
How did you pet her?	Rub, rub, rub.
How did you pet her?	Rub, rub, rub.
Did my cow get sick?	Yes, ma'am.
Was she covered with ticks?	Yes, ma'am.
How did she sound?	Ugh, ugh, ugh.
How did she sound?	Ugh, ugh, ugh.
Did the buzzards come?	Yes, ma'am.
Oh, did the buzzards come?	Yes, ma'am.
How did they come?	Flop, flop, flop.
How did they come?	Flop, flop, flop.
So, what did you do?	Shoo! Shoo! Shoo!
Oh, what did you do?	Shoo! Shoo! Shoo!
Did my cow get better?	Yes, ma'am.
I'm so glad she's better!	Me, too!

Did You Find My Cow?

Adapted by Dr. Maggie

Name_____

Did you find my cow?
Yes, ma'am.
Could you tell me how?
Yes, ma'am.
Where did you find her?
Down in a ditch.

1

Did her legs seem hurt?
Yes, ma'am.
Were they covered with dirt?
Yes, ma'am.
What did she say?
Moo, moo, moo.

2

Did you pet her good?
Yes, ma'am.
Did you pet her like you should?
Yes, ma'am.
How did you pet her?
Rub, rub, rub.

3

Did my cow get sick?
Yes, ma'am.
Was she covered with ticks?
Yes, ma'am.
How did she sound?
Ugh, ugh, ugh.

4

Did the buzzards come?
Yes, ma'am.
Oh, did the buzzards come?
Yes, ma'am.
How did they come?
Flop, flop, flop.

5

So, what did you do?
Shoo! Shoo! Shoo!
Oh, what did you do?
Shoo! Shoo! Shoo!

6

Did my cow get better?
Yes, ma'am.
I'm so glad she's better! *Me, too!*

7

Roles: Group 1, Group 2, Group 3, and Solo

Reproducibles: Pages 122 and 124

Nobody Likes Me!

Adapted by Dr. Maggie

Group 1: Nobody likes me!

Group 2: Everybody hates me!

Group 3: Think I'll go eat worms.

Group 1: Long, thin, slimy ones.

Group 2: Short, fat, juicy ones.

Group 3: Itsy-bitsy, fuzzy-wuzzy worms.

Group 1: Gulp! Down goes the first one.

Group 2: Gulp! Down goes the second one.

Group 3: Gulp! Oh, how they wiggle and squirm!

Group 1: Long, thin, slimy ones.

Group 2: Short, fat, juicy ones.

Group 3: Itsy-bitsy, fuzzy-wuzzy worms.

Group 1: Whoops! Up comes the first one.

Group 2: Whoops! Up comes the second one.

Group 3: Whoops! Too many wiggles and squirms!

Group 1: No more long, thin, slimy ones.

Group 2: No more short, fat, juicy ones.

Group 3: No more itsy-bitsy, fuzzy-wuzzy worms!

Solo: Hey, everybody! I like you! Do you like me? I want to be your friend! Okay?

Nobody Likes Me!

Adapted by Dr. Maggie

Name_____

Jingle Jangles © 2004 Creative Teaching Press

Nobody likes me!
Everybody hates me!
Think I'll go eat worms.

1

Long, thin, slimy ones.
Short, fat, juicy ones.
Itsy-bitsy, fuzzy-wuzzy worms.

2

Gulp! Down goes the first one.
Gulp! Down goes the second one.
Gulp! Oh, how they wiggle
and squirm!

3

Long, thin, slimy ones.
Short, fat, juicy ones.
Itsy-bitsy, fuzzy-wuzzy worms.

4

Whoops! Up comes the first one.
Whoops! Up comes the second one.
Whoops! Too many wiggles
and squirms!

5

No more long, thin, slimy ones.
No more short, fat, juicy ones.
No more itsy-bitsy,
fuzzy-wuzzy worms!

6

Hey, everybody!
I like you! Do you like me?
I want to be your friend! Okay?

7

Roles: Reader 1 and Reader 2

Reproducible: Page 123

Michael Finnegan
Adapted by Dr. Maggie

Reader 1

There was a man
He had whiskers
He shaved
Along came the wind
Poor old Michael Fin-ne-gan.

There was a man
He went fishing
Caught a fish
Poor old Michael Fin-ne-gan.

There was a man
He kicked up
Because they said
Poor old Michael Fin-ne-gan.

Reader 2

named Michael Fin-ne-gan.
on his chin-ne-gan.
them off …
and blew them in again.
Begin again.

named Michael Fin-ne-gan.
with a pin-ne-gan.
and dropped it in again.
Begin again.

named Michael Fin-ne-gan.
an awful din-ne-gan.
he must not sing again.
This is the end!

Michael Finnegan

Adapted by Dr. Maggie

Name_____

Jingle Jangles © 2004 Creative Teaching Press

There was a man
named Michael Fin-ne-gan.
He had whiskers
on his chin-ne-gan.
He shaved them off . . .

1

Along came the wind
and blew them in again.
Poor old Michael Fin-ne-gan.
Begin again.

2

There was a man
named Michael Fin-ne-gan.
He went fishing
with a pin-ne-gan.

3

Caught a fish
and dropped it in again.
Poor old Michael Fin-ne-gan.
Begin again.

4

There was a man
named Michael Fin-ne-gan.
He kicked up
an awful din-ne-gan.

5

STOP!

Because they said
he must not sing again.

6

Poor old Michael Fin-ne-gan.
This is the end!

7

She'll Be Coming 'Round the Mountain

Adapted by Dr. Maggie

Group 1: She'll be coming 'round the mountain
Group 2: when she comes.
Group 3: Toot! Toot!

Group 1: She'll be coming 'round the mountain
Group 2: when she comes.
Group 3: Toot! Toot!

Group 1: She'll be coming 'round the mountain.
Group 2: She'll be coming 'round the mountain.

Group 1: She'll be coming 'round the mountain
Group 2: when she comes.
Group 3: Toot! Toot!

Group 1: She'll be driving six white horses
Group 2: when she comes.
Group 3: Whoa, back!

Group 1: She'll be driving six white horses
Group 2: when she comes.
Group 3: Whoa, back!

Group 1: She'll be driving six white horses.
Group 2: She'll be driving six white horses.

Group 1: She'll be driving six white horses
Group 2: when she comes.
Group 3: Whoa, back! Toot! Toot!

Group 1: Oh, we'll all go out to meet her
Group 2: when she comes.
Group 3: Hi, Babe!

Group 1: Oh, we'll all go out to meet her
Group 2: when she comes.
Group 3: Hi, Babe!

Group 1: Oh, we'll all go out to meet her.
Group 2: Oh, we'll all go out to meet her.

Group 1: Oh, we'll all go out to meet her
Group 2: when she comes.
Group 3: Hi, Babe! Whoa, back! Toot! Toot!

Group 1: She'll be wearing red pajamas
Group 2: when she comes.
Group 3: Scratch! Scratch!

Group 1: She'll be wearing red pajamas
Group 2: when she comes.
Group 3: Scratch! Scratch!

Group 1: She'll be wearing red pajamas.
Group 2: She'll be wearing red pajamas.

Group 1: She'll be wearing red pajamas
Group 2: when she comes.
Group 3: Scratch! Scratch! Hi, Babe!
Whoa, back! Toot! Toot!

Group 1: She will have to sleep with Grandma
Group 2: when she comes.
Group 3: Snee, snore!

Group 1: She will have to sleep with Grandma
Group 2: when she comes.
Group 3: Snee, snore!

Group 1: She will have to sleep with Grandma.
Group 2: She will have to sleep with Grandma.

Group 1: She will have to sleep with Grandma
Group 2: when she comes.
Group 3: Snee, snore! Scratch! Scratch!
Hi, Babe! Whoa, back! Toot! Toot!

She'll Be Coming 'Round the Mountain

Adapted by Dr. Maggie

Name_____

Jingle Jangles © 2004 Creative Teaching Press

She'll be coming
'round the mountain
when she comes. Toot! Toot!
She'll be coming
'round the mountain
when she comes. Toot! Toot!

1

She'll be driving six white horses
when she comes. Whoa, back!
She'll be driving six white horses
when she comes. Whoa, back!
Toot! Toot!

2

Oh, we'll all go out to meet her
when she comes. Hi, Babe! Oh,
we'll all go out to meet her
when she comes. Hi, Babe!
Whoa, back! Toot! Toot!

3

She'll be wearing red pajamas
when she comes. Scratch! Scratch!
She'll be wearing red pajamas
when she comes.

4

Scratch! Scratch! Hi, Babe!
Whoa, back! Toot! Toot!

5

She will have to sleep
with Grandma
when she comes. Snee, snore!
She will have to sleep
with Grandma
when she comes. Snee, snore!

6

She will have to sleep
with Grandma
when she comes.
Snee, snore! Scratch!
Scratch! Hi, Babe! Whoa, back!
Toot! Toot!

7

Roles: Group 1, Group 2, and Solo

Reproducibles: Pages 122 and 124

The Smile of the Crocodile

Adapted by Dr. Maggie

Group 1: She sailed away
Group 2: on a sunny, summer day

Group 1: on the back of a crocodile.

Solo: "You see,"

Group 2: said she,

Solo: "He's as gentle as can be!
Think I'll ride him down the Nile."

Group 1: Then the croc winked his eye

Group 2: as she waved to them good-bye.

Group 1: On his face there was a smile.
At the end of the ride

Group 2: the lady was inside.

Group 1: And the smile

Group 2: was on the crocodile!

The Smile of the Crocodile

Adapted by Dr. Maggie

Name_____

Jingle Jangles © 2004 Creative Teaching Press

She sailed away
on a sunny, summer day

1

on the back of a crocodile.
"You see," said she,

2

"He's as gentle as can be!
Think I'll ride him down the Nile."

3

Then the croc winked his eye
as she waved to them good-bye.

4

On his face there was a smile.

5

At the end of the ride
the lady was inside.

6

And the smile
was on the crocodile!

7

Bill Grogan's Goat

Adapted by Dr. Maggie

Solo Reader

Bill Grogan's goat
was feeling fine.
Ate three red shirts
right off the line.

Bill Grogan tugged
on that goat's back.
Pretended to tie him
to a railroad track.

Now, as that train
drove into sight,
the goat grew pale
and green with fright.

Echo Reader(s)

Bill Grogan's goat
was feeling fine.
Ate three red shirts
right off the line.

Bill Grogan tugged
on that goat's back.
Pretended to tie him
to a railroad track.

Now, as that train
drove into sight,
the goat grew pale
and green with fright.

Jingle Jangles © 2004 Creative Teaching Press

Solo Reader

The goat then sighed
as if in pain.
Coughed up the shirts
and flagged the train!

Bill Grogan smiled.
Oh, please take note.
For he never would
have hurt that goat.

Echo Reader(s)

The goat then sighed
as if in pain.
Coughed up the shirts
and flagged the train!

Bill Grogan smiled.
Oh, please take note.
For he never would
have hurt that goat.

Bill Grogan's Goat

Adapted by Dr. Maggie

Name_____

Jingle Jangles © 2004 Creative Teaching Press

Bill Grogan's goat
was feeling fine.

1

Ate three red shirts right off
the line.

2

Bill Grogan tugged on that
goat's back.

3

Pretended to tie him to a railroad track.

4

Now, as that train drove into sight, the goat grew pale and green with fright.

5

The goat then sighed as if in pain. Coughed up the shirts and flagged the train!

6

Bill Grogan smiled. Oh, please take note. For he never would have hurt that goat.

7

Roles: Group 1 and Group 2

Reproducible: Page 124

Big Rock Candy Mountain

Adapted by Dr. Maggie

Group 1: In the Big Rock Candy Mountain

Group 2: there's a land that's fair and bright.

Group 1: Where the handouts grow on bushes,

Group 2: and you sleep out every night.

Group 1: Where the boxcars all are empty,

Group 2: and the sun shines every day.

Group 1: Oh, I'm bound to go where there isn't any snow,

Group 2: where the rain doesn't fall,

Group 1: and the wind doesn't blow

Group 2: in the Big Rock Candy Mountain.

Group 1: Oh, the buzzin' of the bees in the sycamore trees

Group 2: 'round the soda water fountain,

Group 1: where the lemonade springs and the bluebird sings

Group 2: in the Big Rock Candy Mountain!

Big Rock Candy Mountain

Adapted by Dr. Maggie

Name_____

In the Big Rock Candy Mountain there's a land that's fair and bright.

1

Where the handouts grow on bushes, and you sleep out every night.

2

Where the boxcars are all empty, and the sun shines every day.

3

Oh, I'm bound to go
where there isn't any snow,
where the rain doesn't fall,

4

and the wind doesn't blow
in the Big Rock Candy Mountain.

5

Oh, the buzzin' of the bees
in the sycamore trees
'round the soda water fountain,

6

where the lemonade springs
and the bluebird sings
in the Big Rock Candy Mountain!

7

Way Down South

Adapted by Dr. Maggie

Solo: Ready to read *Way Down South*?
             Take it away, Group 1!

(Note: Group 1 starts and continues chanting while
        Groups 2 and 3 read.)

Group 1: Hay, dee,
             hi, dee,
             ho, dee, who?

Group 2: Way down south
Group 3: where bananas grow,

Group 2: a grasshopper stepped
Group 3: on an elephant's toe.

Group 2: The elephant said with tears in his eyes,
Group 3: "Pick on somebody your own size!"

(All three groups stop together.)

Solo: We've been down south. Let's head out west!
             Then you can decide if west is best!

(Note: Group 1 starts and continues chanting while
        Groups 2 and 3 read.)

Group 1: Hay, hay,
hee, hee,
hi, ho, who?

Group 2: Way out west
Group 3: where cactus grows,

Group 2: a scorpion stepped
Group 3: on an armadillo's toes.

Group 2: The armadillo said with tears in her eyes,
Group 3: "Pick on somebody your own size!"

(All three groups stop together.)

Solo: So . . .
The moral of this story is . . .
girls and guys . . .

**Groups
1, 2, 3:** Picking on another hurts—
whatever the size!

Way Down South

Adapted by Dr. Maggie

Name_____

**Hay, dee,
hi, dee,
ho, dee, who?
This is a story just for you!**

1

**Way down south
where bananas grow,
a grasshopper stepped
on an elephant's toe.**

2

**The elephant said
with tears in his eyes,
"Pick on somebody
your own size!"**

3

We've been down south.
Let's head out west!
Read to find out
if west is best.

4

Way out west
where cactus grows,
a scorpion stepped
on an armadillo's toes.

5

The armadillo said
with tears in her eyes,
"Pick on somebody
your own size!"

6

The moral of this story is,
girls and guys . . .
picking on another hurts—
whatever the size!

7

Roles: Group 1, Group 2, and Solo

Reproducibles: Pages 122 and 124

The Humpty Dumpty Rap

Adapted by Dr. Maggie

(Note: Read to a rhythmic, rap beat.)

Group 1: Humpty Dumpty

Group 2: sat on a wall.

Group 1: Humpty Dumpty

Group 2: had a great fall.

Group 1: All the king's horses

Group 2: and all the king's men

Group 1: couldn't put Humpty

Group 2: together again.

Solo: Who?

Group 1: Humpty Dumpty.

Solo: Describe him.

Group 2: An egg.

Solo: What happened?

Group 1: Humpty Dumpty didn't think at all.
He tried to climb up and sit on a wall.

Group 2: He lost his balance, and then he fell.
He rolled down the wall and started to yell.

Group 1: He hit the ground with a terrible smack!
His brittle white shell really started to crack.

Solo: So what happened then?
Did all the king's horses and all the
king's men ever put Humpty together again?

Group 2: No!

Solo: Why not?

Group 1: He was an egg! A brittle egg!
He was a breakable, unmendable egg!

Group 2: That's right!
Just an egg! A brittle egg!
A breakable, unmendable egg!

Solo: Too bad!

Group 1: So sad!

Solo: Too bad!

Group 2: So sad!

**Solo,
Groups
1 & 2:** FOR HUMPTY!

The Humpty Dumpty Rap

Adapted by Dr. Maggie

Name_____

Humpty Dumpty
sat on a wall.
Humpty Dumpty
had a great fall.

1

All the king's horses
and all the king's men
couldn't put Humpty
together again.

2

Who?
Humpty Dumpty.
Describe him.
An egg.
What happened?

3

He tried to climb up and
sit on a wall.
He lost his balance,
and then he fell.
He rolled down the wall
and started to yell.

4

He hit the ground with
a terrible smack!
His brittle white shell
really started to crack.

5

So what happened then?

So what happened then?
Did all the king's horses
and all the king's men
ever put Humpty together again?

6

No!
Why not?
He was an egg! A brittle egg!
He was a breakable,
unmendable egg!
Too bad! So sad. Too bad!
So sad for Humpty!

7

Roles: Reader 1 and Reader 2

Reproducible: Page 123

A Shoe-Full!

Adapted by Dr. Maggie

Reader 1

There was a kind woman
She had so many children
She gave them some soup
She hugged them all soundly

And then the kind woman
went to feed the cats,
She gave them some food
Then the tired, kind woman

She put on her slippers
She ate a small snack
She checked on the children
So the tired, kind woman
Zzzzzzzzzzzzzzzz!

Reader 2

who lived in a shoe.
she knew what to do.
and a big piece of bread.
and sent them to bed.

with children in bed
Siam and Big Red.
and a fuzzy toy mouse.
went back in the house.

and put up her feet.
of crackers and meat.
but did not hear a peep.
soon fell fast asleep!
Zzzzzzzzzzzzzzzz!

A Shoe-Full!

Adapted by Dr. Maggie

Name_____

There was a kind woman
who lived in a shoe.
She had so many children
she knew what to do.

1

She gave them some soup
and a big piece of bread.
She hugged them all soundly
and sent them to bed.

2

And then the kind woman
with children in bed
went to feed the cats,
Siam and Big Red.

3

She gave them some food
and a fuzzy toy mouse.
Then the tired, kind woman
went back in the house.

4

She put on her slippers
and put up her feet.
She ate a small snack
of crackers and meat.

5

Then she checked on the children
but did not hear a peep.

6

So the tired, kind woman
soon fell fast asleep!
Zzzzzzzzzzzzzzzzz!

7

Roles: Group 1, Group 2, and Solos—Mary, Dottie, Sandra, Maggie

Reproducibles: Pages 124 and 128

Miss Mary Mack and Friends

Adapted by Dr. Maggie

Mary: Welcome to my tea party!
Let's play dress-up. I will wear the black dress.

Dottie: I want to wear that crown!
Sandra: I will wear the shiny red, white, and blue gown!
Maggie: Can't we just go outside and play?

Mary: Maybe later.
Now, we are going to play dress-up!
Why don't you wear the long gray dress?

Maggie: Okay, okay!
Mary: Girls, are you all ready? Lights, camera, action!

Group 1: And now, the fashion show begins!
Group 2: Miss Mary Mack,
Mack, Mack.

Group 1: All dressed in black, black, black.
Group 2: With silver buttons, buttons, buttons.

Group 1: All down her back, back, back.
Group 2: And now . . . Miss Mary Mack's friends!

Group 1: Miss Dottie Downe, Downe, Downe.
Group 2: All dressed in brown, brown, brown.

Group 1: With curly hair, hair, hair.
Group 2: And a silver crown, crown, crown.

Group 1: Miss Sandra Sue, Sue, Sue.
Group 2: All dressed in blue, blue, blue.

Group 1: And red and white, white, white.
Group 2: Lights up the night, night, night.

Group 1: Miss Maggie May, May, May.
Group 2: All dressed in gray, gray, gray.

Group 1: What can we say, say, say?
Group 2: She wants to play, play, play!

Group 1: So all the girls, girls, girls.
Group 2: Took down their curls, curls, curls.

Group 1: Put away each thing, thing, thing.
Group 2: Went outside to swing, swing, swing!

(Mary smiles at Maggie May and gently teases her friend.
Her friend answers with a tease of her own!)

Mary: Okay, Maggie May, May, May.
Are you happy now, now, now?

Maggie: Thank you! Yes, I am, am, am.
Thank you, Mary ma'am, ma'am, ma'am!

Miss Mary Mack and Friends

Adapted by Dr. Maggie

Name_____

Jingle Jangles © 2004 Creative Teaching Press

"Welcome to my tea party!
Let's play dress-up,"
said Mary Mack.
"Can't we just go outside
and play?"
asked Maggie May.

1

"Why don't you wear the
long gray dress?"
"Okay, okay!" said Maggie May.
"Girls, are you all ready?"
asked Mary Mack.
"And now, the fashion
show begins!"

2

Miss Mary Mack, Mack, Mack.
All dressed in black, black, black.
With silver buttons,
buttons, buttons.
All down her back, back, back.

3

And now . . .
Miss Mary Mack's friends!
Miss Dottie Downe,
Downe, Downe.
All dressed in brown,
brown, brown.
And a silver crown, crown, crown.

4

Miss Sandra Sue, Sue, Sue.
All dressed in blue, blue, blue.
And red and white, white, white.
Lights up the night, night, night.

5

Miss Maggie May, May, May.
All dressed in gray, gray, gray.
What can we say, say, say?
She wants to play, play, play!

6

So all the girls, girls, girls.
Took down their curls, curls, curls.
Put away each thing, thing, thing.
Went outside to swing,
swing, swing!

7

Roles: Group 1, Group 2, and Group 3

Reproducible: Page 124

Old Chisholm Trail

Adapted by Dr. Maggie

Group 1: Come along friends. Listen to my tale.

Group 2: I'll tell you my troubles on the old Chisholm Trail.

Group 3: Come-a ti yi yippy, yippy, yay, yippy yay! Come-a ti yi yippy, yippy, yay!

Group 1: On a ten-dollar horse and a forty-dollar saddle,

Group 2: I started out a-punchin' those long-horned cattle.

Group 3: Come-a ti yi yippy, yippy, yay, yippy yay! Come-a ti yi yippy, yippy, yay!

Group 1: I'm up in the morning before daylight.

Group 2: Before I get to sleep the moon's shining bright.

Group 3: Come-a ti yi yippy, yippy, yay, yippy yay! Come-a ti yi yippy, yippy, yay!

Group 1: It's bacon and beans most every day.

Group 2: I'd sooner be eatin' the prairie hay.

Group 3: Come-a ti yi yippy, yippy, yay, yippy yay!
Come-a ti yi yippy, yippy, yay!

Group 1: I'll sell my outfit as soon as I can,

Group 2: 'Cause I'm tired of punchin' cattle
for the big boss man.

Group 3: Come-a ti yi yippy, yippy, yay, yippy yay!
Come-a ti yi yippy, yippy, yay!

Group 1: With my knees in the saddle,
my seat in the sky,

Group 2: I'll quit punchin' cattle in the
sweet by and by.

Group 3: Come-a ti yi yippy, yippy, yay, yippy yay!
Come-a ti yi yippy, yippy, yay!

Old Chisholm Trail

Adapted by Dr. Maggie

Name_____

Jingle Jangles © 2004 Creative Teaching Press

Come along friends,
listen to my tale.
I'll tell you my troubles
on the old Chisholm Trail.

1

On a ten-dollar horse
and a forty-dollar saddle,
I started out a-punchin'
those long-horned cattle.

2

I'm up in the morning
before daylight.
Before I get to sleep
the moon's shining bright.
Come-a ti yi yippy, yippy,
yay, yippy yay!

3

It's bacon and beans
most every day.
I'd sooner be eatin'
the prairie hay.
Come-a ti yi yippy, yippy,
yay, yippy yay!
Come-a ti yi yippy, yippy, yay!

4

I'll sell my outfit as soon as I can,
'cause I'm tired of punchin'
cattle for the big boss man.
Come-a ti yi yippy, yippy, yay,
yippy yay!

5

With my knees in the saddle,
my seat in the sky,
I'll quit punchin' cattle
in the sweet by and by.

6

I said,
"Come-a ti yi yippy, yippy, yay,
yippy yay!
Come-a ti yi yippy, yippy, yay!"

7

Hush, My Children

Adapted by Dr. Maggie

Child 1: Mom, I can't go to sleep!

Child 2: Me either! Please tell us a story.

Child 1: Yes, p-l-e-a-s-e!

Mom: Okay, if you promise to go to sleep,
I'll tell you about Daddy's big surprise.

Child 2: We promise!

Mom: Settle down. Snuggle in. Shhhh!
Hush, my children, don't say a word.
Daddy's going to buy you a mockingbird.

Child 1: A mockingbird? What if it won't sing?

Mom: And if that mockingbird won't sing,
Daddy's going to buy you a diamond ring.

Child 2: A diamond ring?

Mom: And if that diamond ring turns brass,
Daddy's going to buy you a looking glass.

Child 1: You mean a mirror?

Mom: Yes, and if that looking glass gets broke,
Daddy's going to buy you a billy goat.

Child 2: That sounds like fun!

Mom: And if that billy goat won't pull,
Daddy's going to buy you a cart and bull.

Child 1: Then what?

Mom: And if that cart and bull turn over,
Daddy's going to buy you a dog named Rover.

Child 2: We LOVE dogs!

Mom: And if that dog named Rover won't bark,
Daddy's going to buy you a horse and cart.

Child 1: Wow! That's great!
But I am getting very sleepy.

Child 2: Me, too.

Mom: Shhhh!
And if that horse and cart fall down,
you'll still be the best little children in town.
Shhhh! Now, go to sleep. Shhhh!

Hush, My Children

Adapted by Dr. Maggie

Name_____

Jingle Jangles © 2004 Creative Teaching Press

Mom, I can't go to sleep!
Me either! Please tell us a story.
Yes, p-l-e-a-s-e!

1

Okay, if you promise to go
to sleep,
I'll tell you about Daddy's
big surprise.
We promise!
Settle down. Snuggle in. Shhhhh!

2

Hush, my children,
don't say a word.
Daddy's going to buy
you a mockingbird.
And if that mockingbird
won't sing,
Daddy's going to buy
you a diamond ring.

3

And if that diamond ring
turns brass,
Daddy's going to buy
you a looking glass.
And if that looking
glass gets broke,
Daddy's going to buy
you a billy goat.

4

And if that billy goat won't pull,
Daddy's going to buy
you a cart and bull.
And if that cart and bull
turn over,
Daddy's going to buy you a
dog named Rover.

5

And if that dog named Rover
won't bark,
Daddy's going to buy you a
horse and cart.
Wow! That's a great story.
But I am getting very sleepy.
Me, too!

6

Good! Shhhh!
And if that horse and cart
fall down,
you'll still be the best little
children in town.
Shhhh! Now, go to sleep. Shhhh!

7

Roles: Mr. Frog, Miss Mouse, Group 1, and Group 2

Reproducibles: Pages 124 and 126

Mr. Frog Went Courtin'

Adapted by Dr. Maggie

Group 1: Mr. Frog went courtin', and he did ride.

Group 2: Um-hm! Um-hm!

Group 1: Mr. Frog went courtin', and he did ride

Group 2: with a sword and a pistol by his side.

Group 1: Um-hm! Um-hm!
He said:

Mr. Frog: Hello, Miss Mouse! Are you within?

Miss Mouse: Yes, sir. Here I sit and spin.

Group 2: He took Miss Mouse upon his knee.
He said:

Mr. Frog: Miss Mouse, will you marry me?

Miss Mouse: Where will the wedding supper be?

Mr. Frog: Way down yonder in a hollow tree.

Group 1: Now, Mr. Frog was dressed in green.
Um-hm! Um-hm!

Group 2: And Miss Mouse looked just like a queen.
Um-hm! Um-hm!

Jingle Jangles © 2004 Creative Teaching Press

Mr. Frog: Welcome, guests. Welcome little white moth.
Please spread out the tablecloth.

Miss Mouse: Welcome guests. Welcome bumblebee.
Please play that fiddle on your knee.

Group 1: The next guest was a little flea.
He did a jig with the bumblebee.

Group 2: The next guest was a pesky old fly.
He ate up all the wedding pie.

Group 1: The next to come in was a little red ant.
She always said, "I can't, I can't!"

Group 2: The next to come in was a fluffy yellow chick.
He ate so much it made him sick.

Mr. Frog: Welcome guests. Welcome old tomcat.
But don't swallow Miss Mouse—
we can't have that!

Miss Mouse: Welcome guests. Welcome big brown snake.
Now don't gulp Mr. Frog when
he swims in the lake!

Mr. Frog: To all our friends in dressy gowns and pants,
welcome here to our wedding dance.

Miss Mouse: Also, friends, there's bread and cheese
on the shelf.
If you're still hungry, please help yourself!
Um-hm! Um-hm!

Mr. Frog Went Courtin'

Adapted by Dr. Maggie

Name_____

Jingle Jangles © 2004 Creative Teaching Press

Mr. Frog went courtin'
and he did ride
with a sword and a pistol
by his side.
He said, "Hello, Miss Mouse.
Are you within?"
"Yes, sir. Here I sit and spin."

1

He took Miss Mouse
upon his knee.
He said, "Miss Mouse,
will you marry me?"
"Where will the
wedding supper be?"
"Way down yonder
in a hollow tree."

2

"Welcome, guests.
Welcome little white moth.
Please spread out the tablecloth."
"Welcome guests.
Welcome bumblebee.
Please play that fiddle
on your knee."

3

The next guest was a little flea.
He did a jig with the bumblebee.
The next guest was a
pesky old fly.
He ate up all the wedding pie.

4

The next to come in was a
little red ant.
She always said,
"I can't, I can't!"
The next to come in was a
fluffy yellow chick.
He ate so much it made him sick.

5

"Welcome guests.
Welcome old tomcat.
Don't swallow Miss Mouse—
we can't have that!"
"Welcome guests.
Welcome big brown snake.
Don't gulp Mr. Frog
when he swims in the lake!"

6

"To all our friends, in dressy
gowns and pants,
welcome here to our
wedding dance."
"Also, there's bread and
cheese on the shelf.
If you're still hungry,
please help yourself!"

7

Jack and Jill's Motion Commotion

Adapted by Dr. Maggie

Introduction

Narrator: Remember Jack? Remember Jill?
They are the children who live near a hill.

Solo: I always thought about Jack and Jill.
I thought about why they went up that hill.

Narrator: Well, think no more.
For now I will tell about their trip up to the well.

The Story Begins

Narrator: The story starts as Jack and Jill wash their dog, Brutus.
Brutus is a big dog. He splashes a lot!
He splashes most of the water out of the tub.

Jack: Hey, Jill. We need more water!
Let's go to the well.
Want to hike up the hill with me?

Jill: That sounds like great exercise.
Sure, I'll go with you.

Jack: Good, then you can carry the bucket!

Jill: Thanks a lot!

Solo: So that's why they went up the hill!
I always wondered about that!

Narrator: Unfortunately, the well was at the top of a hill.
The hill was steep and rocky.
And, it was very slippery that time of the year.

Jill: Hey, Jack. This is a real power walk!
I don't know if I can keep up with you,
since you had me hold this heavy bucket!
Remember?

Jack: Don't worry, Jill. I'll wait for you at the top.
I'll get the water. Then we can
hike down together.
I'll even carry the bucket for you—
part of the way, that is!

Narrator: And with that, Jack spun around to wink at Jill.

Jill: Thanks a lot, Jack!

Solo: I think Jack was teasing Jill.

Narrator: He was. But, just then, Jack's foot got caught
under a large, jagged rock.
He lost his balance. He started to fall!

Solo: Oh, no!

Jack: Watch out, Jill! H-E-L-P!

Narrator: As Jack tumbled down the hill,
Jill saw him falling toward her.
But she could not move fast enough.

Jill: Oh, no-o-o-o-o!!!

Narrator: Jack fell into Jill. Then they both
fell down the hill.
Down, down, down, all the way
to the bottom of the hill.

Jack & Jill: H-E-L-P!

Narrator: Brutus, the dog, was asleep at the bottom
of the hill.
The falling-down motion caused such
commotion, he woke up.
He moved out of the way just in time.
Boom! Jack and Jill hit the bottom of the hill!

Solo: I bet that hurt!

Jack: Ouch! My head! That really hurt!

Jill: I feel dizzy!

Narrator: Brutus ran over to Jack and Jill.
He looked at their scratches and cuts.
Then he started licking Jack and Jill.

Jack: Gee, what a day!
We just wanted to give Brutus a bath.

Jill: Yes, but it looks like he is giving us one instead!

Jingle Jangles © 2004 Creative Teaching Press

Jack and Jill's Motion Commotion

Adapted by Dr. Maggie

Name_____

Jack and Jill wash
their dog, Brutus.
He splashes most of the
water out of the tub.
"Hey, Jill," said Jack.
"We need more water!
Let's go to the well."

1

"You can carry the bucket!"
said Jack.
"Thanks a lot!" said Jill.
The well was at the
top of a steep hill.
The hill was rocky and slippery.

2

"Hey, Jack," said Jill.
"I don't know if I
can keep up with you."
"Don't worry, Jill," said Jack.
"I'll wait for you at the top.
I'll get the water."

3

I'll even carry the
bucket for you—
part of the way!"
Just then, Jack lost his balance.
He started to fall!

4

"Watch out, Jill! H-E-L-P!"
Jack cried.
Jack tumbled down the
hill toward Jill.
But she could not move
fast enough.
Jack fell into Jill.
They both fell down the hill.

5

Boom! Jack and Jill hit
the bottom of the hill!
"Ouch! My head!
That really hurt!" said Jack.
Jill said, "I feel dizzy!"

6

Brutus licked their
scratches and cuts.
"Gee, what a day!
We just wanted to give
Brutus a bath," said Jack.
"It looks like he is giving
us one instead!"

7

Child 1

Child 2

Frog 1

Frog 2

Solo

Jingle Jangles © 2004 Creative Teaching Press

Echo

Jingle Jangles © 2004 Creative Teaching Press

Farmer

Jingle Jangles © 2004 Creative Teaching Press

Rabbit

Jingle Jangles © 2004 Creative Teaching Press

Girl

Boy

Cat

Dog

Group 1

Group 2

Group 3

Leader

Group A

Group B

Group C

Narrator

Duck

Hen

Mr. Frog

Miss Mouse

Jack

Jingle Jangles © 2004 Creative Teaching Press

Jill

Jingle Jangles © 2004 Creative Teaching Press

Mom

Jingle Jangles © 2004 Creative Teaching Press

Dad

Jingle Jangles © 2004 Creative Teaching Press

Mary

Dottie

Sandra

Maggie